An Angel a Week

An Angel a Week

BALLANTINE BOOKS
NEW YORK

Compilation copyright © 1992 by
Random House, Inc.

All rights reserved under International and Pan-American Copyright Conventions. Published in the United States by Ballantine Books, a division of Random House, Inc., New York, and simultaneously in Canada by Random House of Canada Limited, Toronto.

Owing to limitations of space, permissions acknowledgments appear at the back of this book.

ISBN: 0-345-38075-4

Cover art: *Cupid*, Marie J. Naylor
(Fine Art Photographic Library, London)

TEXT DESIGN BY DEBBY JAY

Manufactured in the United States of America

First Edition: October 1992

10 9 8 7

An Angel a Week

Twice or thrice had I loved thee,
Before I knew thy face or name;
So in a voice, so in a shapeless
      flame,
Angels affect us oft, and worshipped
      be . . .

      —JOHN DONNE,
        "Air and Angels"

Round us, too, shall angels shine,
such as ministered to thee.

—GEORGE HUNT SMYTTEN
"Forty Days and Forty Nights"

Yet I am the necessary angel of
    earth,
Since, in my sight, you see the
    earth again . . .

—WALLACE STEVENS
"Angel Surrounded by Paysans"

Maybe other angels have dropped into other Elm Street backyards? Be-hind fences, did neighbors help earlier hurt ones? Folks keep so much of the best stuff quiet, don't they

—ALLAN GURGANUS
"It Had Wings"

And yet, as angels in some brighter
    dreams
Call to the soul when man doth
    sleep,
So some strange thoughts transcend
    our wonted themes,
And into glory peep.

      —HENRY VAUGHAN
      "They Are All Gone"

Angels descending, bringing
from above,
Echoes of mercy, whispers of
love.

—FANNY J. CROSBY
"Blessed Assurance"

Unless you can love, as the angels
    may,
With the breadth of heaven betwixt
    you;
Unless you can dream that his faith is
    fast,
Through behoving and unbehoving;
Unless you can die when the dream is
    past—
Oh, never call it loving!

      —ROBERT BROWNING
      "A Woman's Shortcomings"

It is wonderful that every angel, in whatever direction he turns his body and face, sees the Lord in front of him.

—EMANUEL SWEDENBORG
The True Christian Religion

We are ne'er like angels till our
passion dies.

—THOMAS DEKKER
"The Honest Whore"

Bless the Lord, ye his angels, that excel in strength, that do his commandments, hearkening unto the voice of his word.

—Psalms, 103:20

Look homeward Angel now,
and melt with ruth

—JOHN MILTON
"Lycidas"

The angels laughed.

God looked down from his seventh heaven and smiled.

The angels spread their wings and, together with Elijah, flew upward into the sky.

—Isaac Bashevis Singer
"Elijah the Slave"

If the archangel, the dangerous one
    behind the stars, took just one
    step down toward us today:
    the quicker pounding of our
    hearts would kill us.

—RAINER MARIE RILKE
    Duino Elegies
    (A. Poulin, Jr., trans.)

We trust in plumed procession
For such the angels go—
Rank after Rank, with even feet—
And uniforms of Snow.

—EMILY DICKINSON
"To fight aloud, is very brave"

Four angels to my bed.
Four angels round my head,
One to watch, and one to pray,
And two to bear my soul away.

—THOMAS ADY
"A Candle in the Dark"

The angels keep their ancient
    places;—
Turn but a stone, and start a
    wing!
'Tis ye, 'tis your estranged faces,
That miss the many-splendoured
    thing.

    —FRANCIS THOMPSON
    "The Kingdom of God"

What is man, that thou art mindful of him? and the son of man, that thou visitest him? For thou hast made him a little lower than the angels, and hast crowned him with glory and honor.

—Psalms 8:4-5

If I have freedom in my love,
    And in my soul am free,
Angels alone that soar above
    Enjoy such liberty.

—RICHARD LOVELACE
"To Althea: From Prison"

Hold the fleet angel fast until he
    blesses thee.

    —NATHANIEL COTTON
        "Tomorrow"

Be not forgetful to entertain strangers, for thereby some have entertained angels unawares.

—Hebrews 13:2

And now it is an angel's song,
That makes the heavens be mute.

—SAMUEL TAYLOR COLERIDGE
"The Rime of the
Ancient Mariner"

Look how the floor of heaven
Is thick inlaid with pattens of
    bright gold.
There's not the smallest orb
    which thou behold'st
But in his motion like an angel
    sings,
Still quiring to the young-ey'd
    cherubins.

—WILLIAM SHAKESPEARE
The Merchant of Venice

Like living flame their faces seemed to
   glow.
Their wings were gold. And all
   their bodies shone
more dazzling white than any
   earthly show.

—DANTE
The Paradiso, Canto XXXI
(John Ciardi trans.)

To transmute a man into an angel was the hope that drove him all over the world and never let him flinch from a meeting or withhold good-byes for long. This hope insistently divided his life into only two parts, journey and rest.

—EUDORA WELTY
"A Still Moment"

For an angel of peace, a faithful guide, a guardian of our souls and bodies, let us entreat the Lord.

—Liturgy of the Eastern
   Orthodox Church

How like an angel came I down!
   How bright are all things here!
When first among his works I did
   appear,
Oh, how their glory did me
   crown!

—THOMAS TRAHERNE
"Wonder"

Tears blinded the tailor's eyes. Was ever man so tried? Should he say he believed a half-drunken Negro to be an angel? . . .

"I think you are an angel from God." He said it in a broken voice, thinking, If you said it it was said. If you believed it you must say it. If you believed, you believed.

—BERNARD MALAMUD
"Angel Levine"

Angels are sweet and sour and salty, wet and dry, hard and soft, sharp and smooth. They fly, yes, but in flights of our own fancy.

—F. FORRESTER CHURCH
Entertaining Angels

It is said by those who ought to understand such things, that the good people, or the fairies, are some of the angels who were turned out of heaven, and who landed on their feet in this world, while the rest of their companions, who had more sin to sink them, went down farther to a worse place.

—WILLIAM BUTLER YEATS
Fairy Tales of Ireland

For he shall give his angels charge over thee to keep thee in all thy ways.

—Psalms 91:2

I arise today:
  in the might of the Cherubim;
  in obedience of Angels;
  in ministration of Archangels.

—SAINT PATRICK
"The Lorica of Saint Patrick"

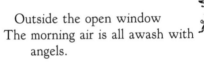

Outside the open window
The morning air is all awash with
    angels.

—RICHARD WILBUR
"Love Calls Us to the Things
of This World"

O, come, angel band,
Come and around me stand,
O, bear me away on your snow
    white wings,
To my immortal home.

—Traditional
"Angel Band"

None sing so wildly well
As the angel Israfel
And the giddy stars (so legends
    tell)
Ceasing their hymns, attend the
    spell
Of his voice, all mute

—EDGAR ALLAN POE
        "Israfel"

. . . all in bright array
The Cherubim descended; on the
    ground
Gliding meteorous, as Ev'ning Mist
Ris'n from a River o'er the marish
    glides,
And gathers ground fast at the
    Laborer's heel
Homeward returning.

       —JOHN MILTON
       Paradise Lost, XII

Sleep, my child, and peace attend
        thee
All through the night.
Guardian angels God will send thee
All through the night.

    —Sir Harold Boulton
    "All Through the Night"

Good-night, sweet prince,
And flights of angels sing thee to
   thy rest!

—WILLIAM SHAKESPEARE
   Hamlet

The soul at its highest is found like God, but an angel gives a closer idea of Him. That is all an angel is: an idea of God.

—MEISTER ECKHART
Sermons

And now were these two men, as
'twere, in Heaven . . . Being swal-
lowed up with the sight of angels,
and with hearing of their melodi-
ous notes.

—JOHN BUNYAN
The Pilgrim's Progress

It is not because angels are holier than men or devils that makes them angels, but because they do not expect holiness from one another, but from God alone.

—WILLIAM BLAKE

Out of the good of evil born,
Came Uriel's voice of cherub
    scorn,
And a blush tinged the upper sky,
And the gods shook, they knew
    not why.

    —RALPH WALDO EMERSON,
      "Uriel"

He'd pass'd the flaming bounds of
    place and time:
The living throne, the sapphire-
    blaze,
Where angels tremble while they
    gaze,
He saw; but, blasted with excess
    of light,
Closed his eyes in endless night.

    —Thomas Gray
    "The Progress of Poesy"

So when the Angel of the darker
    Drink
At last shall find you by the river-
    brink,
  And, offering his Cup, invite your
    Soul
Forth to your Lips to quaff—you shall
    not shrink.

        —EDWARD FITZGERALD
    "Rubaiyat of Omar Khayyam"

At the round earth's imagined
    corners, blow
Your trumpets, angels, and arise,
    arise
From death, you numberless
    infinities
Of souls, and to your scattered
    bodies go . . .

       —JOHN DONNE
       "Divine Meditations"

Gabriel blew, and a clean, thin sound of perfect pitch and crystalline delicacy filled all the universe to the farthest star. As it sounded, there was a tiny moment of stasis as thin as the line separating past from future, and then the fabric of the worlds collapsed upon itself. . . . The Last Trump had sounded."

—ISAAC ASIMOV
"The Last Trump"

And the angel said unto her, Fear not, Mary: for thou hast found favor with God. And, behold, though shalt conceive in thy womb, and bring forth a son, and shalt call his name Jesus.

—Luke 1:30

Angels and archangels may have
    gathered there,
Cherubim and seraphim thronged
    the air;
But his mother only, in her madien
    bliss,
Worshipped the beloved with a kiss.

      —CHRISTINA ROSSETTI
      "In the Bleak Mid-Winter"

The angels sing the praise of their
Lord and ask forgiveness for
those on earth . . .

    —The Qur'an XLII:5

And the angel said unto them, Fear not: for, behold, I bring you good tidings of great joy, which shall be to all people.

—Luke 2:10

Angels, we have heard on high
Singing sweetly through the night,
And the mountains in reply
Echoing their brave delight.

　　　—French Christmas carol

All God's angels come to us
disguised.

—James Russell Lowell
"On the Death of a
Friend's Child"

Praised be all the angels
for ever.

—Tobit, 11:15